The Simple Guide to a Minimalist Life

by

Leo Babauta

The Simple Guide to a Minimalist Life

ISBN 1-4495568-2-5

Table of Contents

dedications

for my children: Chloe, Justin, Rain, Maia, Seth and Noelle.

also for Guampedia.com.

A small irony

Yes, I know it's ironic that a book on minimalism is more than a page or two long. The content isn't minimalist, and that's contradictory, right?

Well, sure. I could do a book that's just a paragraph long. But would that be worth your time and money? Would it help you achieve what you came here for?

I wanted to create a really useful guide, and so that means I've put a "more than minimal" amount of information into this book. I hope that's good for you. If not, delete the book now!

Notes on using this book

The first thing to note is that this isn't a step by-step guide that you should follow from beginning to end.

It's a series of guides on different areas that can help you explore a life of minimalism. There is no one single path -- yours will be different than mine, and I can't prescribe exact steps you should take.

I share my experiences and what I've learned in hopes that it'll help you.

Second note is some will notice that not everything in this book is new material. Some is new, but much is gathered from various writings I've made on these topics around the web. I highly doubt that anyone reading this book has read all the articles previously published -- they've been widely scattered, and over a long period of time.

Even still, I've updated and expanded on previous writings, and I've added some new content. I've put it all together in hopes that it'll save you some time searching for good articles on these topics.

Use this as a reference guide that you refer back to, because on your journey you'll find new things on each reading, as you go through this process. I hope it'll be a useful guide on this journey.

What is a minimalist life?

"Be Content with what you have; rejoice in the way things are. When you realize there is nothing lacking, the whole world belongs to you."
- Lao Tzu

It's one that is stripped of the unnecessary, to make room for that which gives you joy.

It's a removal of clutter in all its forms, leaving you with peace and freedom and lightness.

A minimalist eschews the mindset of more, of acquiring and consuming and shopping, of bigger is better, of the burden of stuff.

A minimalist instead embraces the beauty of less, the aesthetic of sparseness, a life of contentedness in what we need and what makes us truly happy.

A minimalist realizes that acquiring stuff doesn't make us happy. That earning more and having more are meaningless. That filling your life with busy-ness and freneticism isn't desirable, but something to be avoided.

A minimalist values quality, not quantity, in all forms.

I'm a minimalist, and it's something that's deeply satisfying. I wake in the morning in a room that lacks clutter, in the quiet of the early morning, have coffee and read, go out for a run, and then write. Work a little more, spend some time with my family.

These are the things that make me happy. Not buying a lot of things. Not traveling all the time, nor going to parties or spending money on expensive entertainment.

Not watching a lot of television and being bombarded with ads. Others might find joy in these things, and I'm not criticizing them. I'm just stating what makes me happy.

And that's the key. Figure out what makes you happy. Get rid of the rest, so you have room for those important things. It's not a life of nothing, of boringness. It's a life of richness, in less.

Your minimalist life will be different than mine. You'll need to figure out what makes you happiest. Plan your ideal day. Then strip your life of the non-essentials, to make room for this ideal day, for the things and people you love. This book is meant to help you find that path.

Overall minimalist principles

"Fear less, hope more; eat less, chew more; whine less, breathe more; talk less, say more; love more, and all good things will be yours."
- Swedish proverb

Minimalism isn't necessarily all about less. It's also not an end in and of itself. It's a path, to help you to:

- Have more freedom
- Have more time
- Have more room for what's important
- Have less worry
- Have more pleasure
- Be more frugal
- Become greener
- Become healthier

The Minimalist Principles

There are some key principles we'll be repeating throughout this book, in various forms. It's important to list them here:

1. **Omit needless things**. Notice this doesn't say to omit everything. Just needless things.

2. **Identify the essential**. What's most important to you? What makes you happy? What will have the highest impact on your life, your career?

3. **Make everything count**. Whatever you do or keep in your life, make it worthy of keeping. Make it really count.

4. **Fill your life with joy**. Don't just empty your life. Put something wonderful in it.

5. **Edit, edit.** Minimalism isn't an end point. It's a constant process of editing, revisiting, editing some more.

In anything you do, see if you can apply these principles. There's no need to get obsessive about it, of course, but it's always useful to examine what we do, how we do it, and whether we really need to do it.

How to become a minimalist

But at the core of things, to become a minimalist, all you need to do is the four things above.
"Great acts are made up of small deeds."
- Lao Tzu

While minimalist aesthetics and products and the minimalist lifestyle appeals to a lot of people, they find it easier to like it than to live it.

Minimalism is something people might strive for, but they don't know where to start. There are lots of things to do, to think about, and it can be overwhelming. Here's where I'd start:

- **Start by realizing you already have enough**.

  We'll look more into this in the next chapter, but this is really key. Being content with what you have is important, or all the decluttering in the world won't matter, because you'll just want more.

- **Start cutting back on clutter and possessions**.

  We'll get into this asap, but really if you have a home or office full of clutter, you're not minimalist yet. We want to get rid of this clutter, and it can be done in a weekend or two, or it can be done slowly over the course of weeks. Either is fine, but the key is to start.

- **Start simplifying your schedule**.

  Cut back on commitments, take the unnecessary stuff out of your schedule, and leave some breathing room. Allow yourself to focus on the important stuff.

- **Slowly edit everything you do**, with minimalist principles in mind. It's a constant process.

That's it. It's pretty simple. We'll go into more depth, of course, covering eating and fitness and finances and family and all of that.

Contentedness: You already have enough

"He who is contented is rich." - Lao Tzu

"The secret of happiness, you see, is not found in seeking more, but in developing the capacity to enjoy less." - Socrates

This is really the starting place. It's not enough to just strip things bare, because clutter will eventually accumulate if you continue to acquire things. And at the root of the desire to acquire is a discontentedness with how things are now.

If you're buying things you don't need, it's because you're dissatisfied in some way. You want more, not just what you have now. You want more excitement, fun, ways to make your life better. You want something cooler. Whatever the reason, you're not happy with what you have.

It's a problem that can go pretty deep, but the solution doesn't have to be complicated.
Here's what I suggest:

1. **Realize you already have all you really need**. What are the things you truly need? Food, water, basic clothing, shelter, loved ones. Everything else is extra. You don't need the latest technology, stylish clothing, cool new shoes, a fancy car, a big house.

2. **Learn to stop buying non-necessities**. This might sound difficult, but it's a matter of being conscious of it. One great method is to start a 30-day list -- make it a rule that if you want to buy a non-necessity, you

have to put it on this list (with the date it was added) and you can't buy it for at least 30 days. If you still want it after 30 days, you can buy it. This usually works, because the urge to buy dissipates. Always ask before buying: Is this an absolute necessity?

3. **Learn to be happy by doing, not owning**. We can be happy with just the true necessities, if we learn that owning things, having things, does not make us happy. Instead, doing things can make us happy -- talking with a friend, taking a walk with a loved one, cooking, creating, singing, running, working on something exciting. If you can focus on doing things that make you happy, you'll have less of a need for stuff.

4. **Learn the concept of Enough**. This is the idea that we don't always need more -- that once we reach a certain point, we have enough. The key is to learn to recognize when that is. Often we don't realize we have enough, and are caught up in the cycle of more.

Having more breeds wanting more. It's an endless cycle of more, an addiction to acquiring and owning. We need to learn when enough is enough, and be happy with what we have.

This doesn't happen overnight. It takes time, but most importantly it takes a consciousness of all of this -- of necessities vs. wants, of more vs. enough, of being happy by doing not owning. Over time, this consciousness will result in a contentedness with what we already have, which is a true foundation for a minimalist life.

Rethinking necessities

"If your mind isn't clouded by unnecessary things, then this is the best season of your life."
- Wu-Men

One of the basics of minimalism is that you eliminate as many non-necessities as you can, to make room for what's important.

If you don't need a ton of clothing, you get rid of much of it. If you don't need that new gadget, you don't buy it. Within reason, of course.

You learn to be content with what you already have, with the necessities, with doing things you love rather than having things.

But it's funny, because often things we assume are necessities are not necessarily so. The problem is that we categorize things as necessities because we're used to them, and we can't see how to live without them. And it's difficult to make big changes.

Some examples:

- **A car**. Cars are seen as necessities, but amazingly, people lived without them for quite awhile before the 20th century. Even today, some people manage to go carless. And it's not impossible — especially if you live in a place with a decent public transportation system. And there are car sharing options now in many cities, so you can use a car when you need it, for much less than actually owning a car. It's possible to bike and walk most places, and take public transit and shared cars everywhere else.

9

- **Meat**. Many people believe they can't live without steaks and burgers. And I was one of them. These days, I'm not only vegetarian, but mostly vegan. And it's not that hard to change, if you do it slowly. It's also healthier and better for the environment — meat and dairy animals are tremendously harmful to the environment and a huge waste of our natural resources.

- **Lots of clothes**. While I don't advocate going naked (though some do it) nor do I recommend just owning one outfit, it is possible to own less clothing than most people have. We don't need to constantly buy clothes to stay fashionable — we can buy quality, timeless clothing, with colors and patterns chosen so that all our clothes go with each other.

- **A big house**. Have less stuff, you need less house.

These are just a few examples — think about all the things you consider necessities. Are they really? What's really needed, beyond food, shelter, basic clothing, and loved ones?

Simplify what you do

It's important, from this point on, to try to say "no" to all requests for commitments if
"Nature does not hurry, yet everything is accomplished."
- Lao Tzu

Living a minimalist life isn't just about eliminating physical clutter. It's about reducing the clutter of your busy schedule, your work life, all the running around you might normally do.

It's about doing only what's necessary, so you have time for what makes you truly happy.

Reduce commitments

The most important thing you can do to simplify your schedule is to list all your commitments, and pick the most important ones. Commitments include everything that takes up your time, from work projects to side jobs to serving on civic committees to coaching for your kids' soccer team to renovating your home to serving on a PTO or other school committee.

These commitments are easy to say "yes" to, but they fill up our lives as they accumulate, until we're so busy we have no time for what's really important to us. Minimalism suggests we reduce these commitment to just the most important, leaving room in our lives for what we love most and leaving space so we're not as stressed out.

To do this, make a list of every commitment you can think of. Anything you do on a regular basis, or that you've committed to doing in the near term or long term.

Now mark this list: what are the 4-5 most important commitments? The things you love most, that are most valuable to you. These are your top priorities. Everything else should be removed, if at all possible.

To remove commitments, you need to make a phone call or send an email informing people that you can no longer commit to something. This is difficult and uncomfortable, because it means saying "no" to people, and often disappointing them. But you know what? They'll live, and their projects and lives will go on. While it's difficult to disappoint people, it's rarely as bad as we fear.

This is a slow process of removal -- there will be some commitments you can't get out of right away. But if you keep in mind that you want to eventually get rid of all non-essential commitments, you'll slowly get out of them, either by saying "no" or when the commitments are finished naturally.

It's important, from this point on, to try to say "no" to all requests for commitments if they're not on your essential list -- things you really love doing. You should want to say "Hell yes" to new commitments -- or say no. Don't just say yes.

Once you've gotten rid of non-essential commitments, your life will be freed to do the things you've always wanted to do.

Clear your schedule

See how clear you can make your schedule. This means cutting back on meetings, which are often a waste of time anyway. It means not making appointments if you can avoid it. It means leaving big blocks of time available for creating, for doing the work you love, for doing other things you love.

Leave space between things in your schedule. The space helps you to go through your schedule with less stress, and if things run long, it won't throw everything off.
If you can, leave entire days without scheduled appointments. That doesn't mean you won't do any work -- it just means nothing is hard-coded into your calendar.

Cut back on your to-do list

If you have a long to-do list filled with lots of things to do, the minimalist way is to simplify the list.

To do this, you must be honest with yourself: can you really do all the things on your to-do list today? How about in the next three days? Often we believe we can do more than we actually can, and as a result we make long to-do lists that we could never do in a day or three.

Now, it's the nature of to-do lists to be never-ending, but the real problem is that they're filled with lots of tasks that keep us super busy. And instead, we should be focusing on fewer tasks, not more.

Fewer tasks means we're less busy. It also means that we must select the most important ones the tasks that will have the highest impact on our work and our lives.

Choose three tasks for each day -- really important, high-impact tasks. These three Most Important Tasks (MITs) should be your focus each day, and ideally you should do them before working on any tasks of lower importance.

Do the important stuff first. Worry about the little things later.

14

On clearing clutter

"Have nothing in your houses that you do not know to be useful, or believe to be beautiful."
- William Morris

Clutter is poison to a minimalist. The minimalist will toss out the unnecessary and be left with sparse beauty.

The problems with clutter:

- stuff weighs you down

- stuff stresses you out

- stuff is expensive, to buy, store and maintain

- looking for stuff in clutter leads to wasted time

- clutter is a reflection of your internal state

You accumulate clutter by being in the mindset of Acquiring rather than a mindset of Enough. You accumulate it by having a fear mentality, not wanting to let go of things, wanting to hoard and keep everything for sentimental reasons.

Being too busy also leads to clutter, because we don't have time to clean up, don't have time to get rid of the unnecessary, and clutter will pile up. So reducing what you do will help clear clutter.

Not having a system for dealing with stuff, and not having the habits to keep the system going, will lead to clutter. You can declutter you home and get it looking beautiful, but if you don't have a system and habits in place, you'll soon start putting things down in any old place, and soon will have clutter again.

The solution is to find a place for everything, once you've done some decluttering. This isn't too hard -- you just need to put something in a place you think is a good "home" for that thing, and then make a mental note of that place. Then you need to get into the habit of putting that thing in its place whenever you're done with it. It takes more time to form that habit, but it's not too difficult if you do it consciously.

Beating the Fear Mentality

So if you're afraid to let go of stuff, how do you conquer that fear in order to declutter?

There are a few related fears or emotions related to keeping stuff:

- Fear of needing it again

- Reluctance to waste something valuable

- Not wanting to let go of sentimental things, because of emotional connection

These are all strong emotions and if they're not addressed, will stop you from decluttering.

Here's how to beat them:

1. **If you haven't used it in 6 months, toss it.** For seasonal items such as winter clothes, extend the rule to 12 months or so. If you don't use it, you don't need it. But what if some occasion comes up where you do need it? Well, that's not likely, but ask yourself what you could do in such an event -- could you use something else instead, or borrow it from someone

else, rent it, or in a worst-case scenario, buy another one (preferably used)? Usually, we can do without it or find another solution, and usually, such a scenario doesn't happen -- as evidenced by not using it for the last 6 months. Sometimes it does, but it's not the end of the world.

2. **It's wasteful to hold on to things.** While I know many people who feel it's wasteful to get rid of things that can still be used -- and part of me strongly agrees with that -- this belief leads to the accumulation of incredible amounts of junk and clutter. I know because I've seen all their clutter. It's not pretty. Instead, realize that it's actually more wasteful to hold on to things if you don't use and love them.

   First, they waste space, which actually costs you money each month (in the form of rent or mortgage of your home, or renting or buying additional storage space).

   It also costs you time to maintain all of the clutter, and stress in maintaining it and see it and going through all of it to find things.

   Finally, if these things are actually still usable and valuable, give them to someone else who can and will use them. Things aren't valuable if they're not used. So by holding onto things, you are preventing them from actually being used by someone who needs them.

3. **Take a picture.** If things have sentimental value, it's because of the memories they hold, not because of what they actually are or what they can be used for. So take a digital picture, or if it's a picture or document, scan it into your computer. You'll still have the memories, but they'll take up no space. Try this, for at least a few things, and you'll see that the sentimental

17

value of things can be moved into the digital space to defeat this fear.

4. **The "maybe" box.** If you just can't bring yourself to get rid of things, have a "maybe" box when you declutter. This is a box for all the things you're on the fence about -- put them into a box, mark the date, and put the box into a closet or other storage. After 6 months, if you never needed these items, get rid of them. This is a stopgap measure designed to overcome these fears.

How to Get Started

Getting started tackling a house full of clutter can be difficult because the task is too overwhelming. It's important, then, to start small.

You don't need to take on the mountain. Just start with one rock at a time.

The Fly Lady (flylady.net) recommends starting with your kitchen sink, and I agree with that. Clear out your sink (wash any dishes), clean it well, and get it nice and shiny. This is something you can do in 5-10 minutes (depending on how many dishes there are), and it has a motivating effect.

Now keep this sink clean and shiny. From here, you can expand: clear your kitchen counters, and wipe them clean. Clear your kitchen floors of clutter. Keep these areas clean for a few days.

Expand to other rooms -- table tops, then floors, then shelves, then closets. One surface at a time. But keep the sink clean, and any areas you've already decluttered and cleaned, keep them clean.

You don't need to tackle all of this overnight. You can do it a little at a time -- 10-15 minutes a day, or more if you like. If you want, you can schedule a weekend of decluttering, but it's not necessary. Gradually, you'll get there.

Decluttering system

Here's a brief system for decluttering:

1. **Start with one flat surface at a time.**
   This can be a countertop, a tabletop, a section of the floor in a room, a shelf, the floor of a closet, a cabinet. Just focus on one shelf in a closet at a time, for example, not the whole closet.

2. **Take everything off the surface (or out of the drawer or cabinet).** Put it all into one big pile. You don't literally have to pile things -- just put them all together, maybe on a table or on the floor, but not on the table or floor you're decluttering. This will be your temporary workspace.

3. **Take one thing off the pile, and make a quick decision with it.** Do you love and use this regularly? Have you used it in the last 6 months? If so, put it in a separate "keep" pile. If not, put it in a "donate" box, or trash or recycle bag if it's actually trash. You can have a third option of a "maybe" box for items you can't decide on -- see the previous section of this chapter for more on that.

4. **Repeat this process with every item in the pile, one at a time, making quick decisions with each item, until you're done.** If you make quick decisions, it doesn't have to take long. You should now have two piles -- a "keep" pile, and a donate box, plus a trash bag. Perhaps also the "maybe" box if you go that route.

5. **Now clean the surface, shelf, cabinet.** Then put back the "keep" pile, neatly and sorted. Put spaces in between stuff. Find other homes for things that don't really belong here.

6. **Put the donate box into your car to be dropped off tomorrow.** Throw out the trash. Put the maybe box, if you used it, into storage. You're done!

Repeat this process for other flat surfaces.

What to do with unneeded stuff

You don't need to actually throw things in the trash when you declutter. There are many options for getting rid of things you don't need or love. Here are a few:

- Donate to Goodwill or other such charities

- Freecycle.org - a site for giving away things to people who need them, in your area

- Have a yard sale

- Sell your stuff on Ebay.com (tip: put your CDs in bundles and sell them)

- Give things to friends and family who need them

- Donate DVDs and books to the library

- Sell books to used bookshops

- Recycle

- Make something out of the items, and give it as a gift

Minimalist home

**"One can furnish a room very luxuriously by taking
out furniture rather than putting it in."**
- Francis Jourdain

I try to keep my home relatively uncluttered -- not
completely empty or sparse, but not cluttered at all.

For example, on the floor of my kitchen/ dining room area
are just a few essentials: dining table (clear of any clutter),
chairs. On the counter is only the coffee maker.

In my living room is only a pair of couches, a TV stand, a
side table, a lamp, and my computer desk and chair. The
desk has only my iMac and keyboard, with no paper files
or other clutter.

I don't see this kind of minimalist home as devoid of
character and fun and life -- instead, I get a kind of
fulfillment at looking around and seeing a home free of
clutter. It's calming, and liberating, and just nice.

Benefits of a Minimalist Home Just a few key benefits:

- **Less stressful**. Clutter is a form of visual distraction,
  and everything in our vision pulls at our attention at
  least a little. The less clutter, the less visual stress we
  have. A minimalist home is calming.

- **More appealing**. Think about photos of homes that
  are cluttered, and photos of minimalist homes. The
  ones with almost nothing in them except some
  beautiful furniture, some nice artwork, and a very few
  pretty decorations, are the ones that appeal to most of

us. You can make your home more appealing by making it more minimalist.

- **Easier to clean**. It's hard to clean a whole bunch of objects, or to sweep or vacuum around a bunch of furniture. The more stuff you have, the more you have to keep clean, and the more complicated it is to clean around the stuff. Think about how easy it is to clean an empty room compared to one with 50 objects in it. That's an extreme example, of course, as I wouldn't recommend you have an empty room, but it's just to illustrate the difference.

What a Minimalist Home Looks Like

This would vary, of course, depending on your taste and how extreme of a minimalist you want to be. I am a minimalist, but not to any extreme. But here are some characteristics of a minimalist home:

* Minimal furniture. A minimalist room would only contain a few essential pieces of furniture. A bedroom, for example, might have a simple bed (or even just a mattress), a dresser, and perhaps a night stand or book shelf.

- **Clear surfaces**. All flat surfaces are clear, except for one or two decorations (see next item). There are not a whole bunch of knick knacks, and definitely not stacks of books or papers or other items.

- **Accent decorations**. A home completely clear of things would be a bit boring, actually. So instead of having a coffee table completely free of any objects, you could have a simple vase with a few flowers, for example. Or a clear desk might just have a family photo. An otherwise empty wall might have a tasteful piece of art (I use my dad's artwork, as he's a great artist).

- **Quality over quantity**. Instead of having a lot of stuff in your home, a minimalist would choose just a few really good things he loves and uses often. A really nice table, for example, is better than 5 pieces of pressboard furniture.

How to Create a Minimalist Home

The real key is to change your philosophy and shoot for the ideals in the previous section above. But here are some tips that I would offer to anyone trying to shoot for minimalism:

- **One room at a time**. Unless you're just moving into a place, it's hard to simplify an entire house at once. Focus on one room, and let that be your center of calm. Use it to inspire you to simplify the next room, and the next. Then do the same outside!

- **Look at the furniture**. The biggest things in any room are the furniture, so you should always begin simplifying a room by looking at the furniture. The fewer pieces of furniture, the better (within reason, of course). Think of which furniture can be eliminated without sacrificing comfort and livability. Go for a few pieces of plain, simple furniture (example of a minimalist coffee table) with solid, subdued colors.

- **Only the essentials**. Whether looking at your furniture or anything else in the room, ask yourself if the item is truly essential. If you can live without it, get it out. Try to strip the room down to its essentials — you can always add a few choice items beyond the essentials later.

- **Clear floors**. Except for the furniture, your floors should be completely clear. Nothing should clutter the floor, nothing should be stacked, nothing should be stored on the floor. Once you've gotten your furniture down to the bare essentials, clear everything else on the floor — either donate it, trash it, or find a place for it out of sight.

- **Store stuff out of sight**. This has been mentioned in the above tips, but you should store everything you need out of sight, in drawers and cabinets. Bookshelves can be used to store books or DVDs or CDs, but shouldn't have much else except a few simple decorations (not whole collections of things).

- **Simple artwork**. To keep a room from being boring, you can put a simple painting, drawing or photo, framed with a subdued, solid color, on each wall if you want. Leave some walls bare if possible.

- **Simple decorations**. One or two simple decorations can serve as accents for a minimalist room. A vase of flowers or a small potted plant are two classic examples. If the rest of your room has subdued colors, your accents could use a bright color (such as red, or yellow) to draw the eye and give a plain room a splash of energy.

- **Plain patterns**. Solid colors are best for floor coverings (if you have any), furniture, etc. Complex patterns, such as flowers or checkers, are visual clutter.

- **Subdued colors**. You can have a splash of bright color in the room, but most of the room should be more subtle colors - white is classic minimalist, but really any solid colors that don't stress the eyes is good (earth colors come to mind, such as blues, browns, tans, greens).

- **Edit and eliminate**. When you've simplified a room, you can probably do more. Give it a couple of days, then look at everything with a fresh eye. What can be eliminated? Stored out of sight? What's not essential? You can come back to each room every few months, and sometimes you'll discover things you can simplify even more.

- **A place for everything**. It's important that you find a place for everything, and remember where those places are. Where does you blender go? Give it a spot, and stick with it. Aim for logical spots that are close to where the thing is used, to make things more efficient, but the key is to designate a spot.

- **Sit back, relax, and enjoy**. Once you've simplified a room, take a moment to look around and enjoy it. It's so peaceful and satisfying. This is the reward for your hard work. Ahhhh. So nice!

The desk and computer I use.

Minimalist workspace

"Our life is frittered away by detail… Simplify, simplify, simplify! … Simplicity of life and elevation of purpose."

- Henry David Thoreau

How minimalist is your workspace? An uncluttered workspace is a thing of beauty.

The definition of a minimalist workspace will be different for each person. The most extreme minimalist workspace, I think, would be to have no desk or papers or computer or anything of the kind — just yourself. You'd think, and talk, and maybe sit on the floor.

Of course, that won't work for most of us, so it's more useful to look at our minimum requirements, and focus on creating a workspace that addresses these essentials and nothing more.

So the first step is for you to consider your requirements for working, and what's essential to your workflow. If possible, streamline and simplify that workflow and those requirements. Then, once you've got that down to a minimum, see what the minimum setup would be for those essentials and your workflow. Eliminate everything unnecessary.

What are your requirements?

It's interesting to note that what you think your requirements are might not be the minimum. They might just be what you're used to doing.

Taking myself as an example: I used to work with tons of paper, files, sticky notes, and all the usual office tools (pens, pencils, notebooks, pads, stapler, hole puncher, whiteout, calendar, personal organizer, etc.). But then I realized that it's possible to work without paper, and I've eliminated the need for all that stuff. In fact, as I've eliminated paper, I've eliminated the need for drawers.

Now, you might not have that luxury, and you might not want to go that extreme. Your needs are different than mine — but the point is to see if it's possible to change the way you work, so that you still get the essentials done, without all the same requirements. It's worth some thought at least — and if you make changes, as I did, you might find that changing things in small increments is better. I didn't do away with paper altogether. I did it in steps, eliminating different needs for paper one at a time.

My Minimalist Setup

Basically, I have an iMac and a very minimalist desk, with no drawers, printer, papers, files, or office tools.

I work from home these days, and I do everything online. I do have a phone (elsewhere in my house, so it doesn't disturb me) and a cell phone (also elsewhere), but I don't have a PDA, an iPod, a printer (though my wife has ordered one for her needs), a scanner, a fax machine, or anything like that. I don't print anything and I don't use fax (an outdated technology).

On my computer, I mostly just use the browser, as I do nearly everything online. I also use text programs for writing and a couple other utilities for uploading files and photo editing.

All my organizing needs are taken care of on the computer: Address Book, Gmail, text files for to-do lists and errands and ideas and projects, Gcal for scheduling.

Tips for Creating Your Own Minimalist Workspace

You won't need to have my setup, but once you've determined your minimum needs, here are some tips for making your workspace as minimalist as possible. Not all tips will work for you, so pick and choose which ones will work best for your workflow.

- **Have one inbox**. If paper is a part of your life, keep an inbox tray on top of your desk and make sure ALL papers, including phone messages and sticky notes, go into this tray. You might have to train your co-workers who put papers on your desk if they're not already used to this. Don't leave papers scattered all over your desk, unless you're actually working on them at this moment. You might also have a "working file" folder for papers you're working on but not at this moment, but put this working file in a drawer, so that it's out of the way.

- **Clear out your inbox each day**. Nothing should go back in there after you process them. It's not a storage bin, but an inbox. To clear your inbox, process top down, one item at a time. Make quick decisions on each item, and take action: file immediately, trash, forward to someone else, take immediate action, or put it on your to-do list and in your action folder to later action.

- **Clear your desk**. Aside from your computer, your inbox tray, your phone, and maybe a nice photo of a loved one, there should be nothing on top of your desk. No papers (again, unless you're working on them), no notes, no stapler or pens or other junk. Clear as much of it off as humanly possible. If you want to include a couple other essentials, you should, but be sure they absolutely must be there. Keep it as clear as possible, as a clear desk is a relaxing workspace. Use the decluttering method in the chapter on Clearing Clutter.

- **Get rid of knick-knacks**. This goes with the above item, but many people don't even think about all the little trinkets they have on top of their desk. They're usually unnecessary. Toss 'em!

- **Clear the walls**. Many people have all kinds of stuff posted on their walls. It creates visual clutter. Get them off your walls. If it's a reference guide, put it on your computer and set up a hotkey so you can call the guide up with a keystroke when needed.

- **Clear your computer desktop**. We'll cover how to keep your computer as minimalist as possible in the next chapter.

- **Re-examine your paper needs**. While you might think the way you do things now is necessary, it's possible you can do things digitally instead of through paper. Give this some serious thinking, and if possible, eliminate paper to the extent you can. It'll give you a more minimalist workspace. More on this in a couple chapters.

- **Eliminate unnecessary tools**. Think about each tool you have in your desk, in your work area, and even in your office. Do you need a stapler and hole puncher? Do you need all those pens? Do you really need a fax machine? Or a scanner? You might not have control over all these types of tools, but if you do, eliminate the ones you don't really need, maybe one at a time.

- **Simplify your filing**. As mentioned above, it's unnecessary to keep paper copies of files you have on your computer or can access online. Back stuff up online if you're worried about losing them. Having stuff digitally makes them searchable, which is much better than filing. Just archive, and search when necessary. If you do need paper files, keep them alphabetically and file immediately, so that you don't have a huge "to be filed" pile. Once every few months, weed out unnecessary files.

- **Go through each drawer**. One drawer at a time, take out all the contents and eliminate everything you don't need. It's much nicer to use drawers if you can open them and see order. Have a designated spot for each item and make sure to put those items back in that spot immediately, every time.

- **Clear the floor**. There should be nothing on your floor but your desk and chair. No files, no boxes. Keep it clear!

My minimalist desktop.

Minimalist computer

"Simplicity is the ultimate sophistication."
- Leonardo da Vinci

A minimalist computer setup, as paradoxical as that may sound to some, lends itself to a more serene, focused creative environment in my experience.

I love a clean desktop, a friction-free interface, and simple tools that help me focus on what I really need to get done: to create, without distractions.

And when I gaze lovingly at my icon-less desktop, I sigh with contentment. I really love simplicity.

An Uncluttered Desktop

I don't have any icons on my computer desktop — I've had the experience of having a thousand icons on the desktop and it really doesn't compare to an uncluttered environment. Sure, it may be easy to just double-click on a frequently used app or document (although that's not as fast as what I suggest under the "Interface" section below). But having to look at so many icons is visual stress and distraction, so I've banished this method of working.

Now, I have zero icons on the desktop and I usually choose a fairly minimalist (but beautiful) desktop pic to complete the experience. See my desktop in the pic above. Here's what to do:

1. Put all icons on your desktop into a folder. You could put them into a "Temp" folder for sorting later, or create two folders and sort them quickly: "Working" and "Archives". Working is for stuff you're working on right now, and Archives is for everything else. More on filing structure below.

2. On the Mac, remove the hard drive icon by selecting "Preferences" (Cmd-,) and under the "General" tab, deselect "Hard disks" under "Show these items on the Desktop". On the PC, you can right-click on the desktop and under the "View" submenu, deselect "Show desktop icons".

3. On the Mac, set the Dock to auto-hide in the Dock preferences. I never use the Dock anymore (see the next section).

4. Choose a serene desktop pic (or "wallpaper"). I like ones with a plain colored background (such as white or black) and a nice minimalist picture on it. Or just a nice nature scene. Nothing too distracting. 5. I also don't like a lot of icons or apps in my menu bar, so I remove everything that isn't necessary. Right now all I have is the clock and Spotlight. On the PC, I do the same thing - remove everything.

Simple Interface

If you're still using the mouse to open programs and documents, you should seriously consider using the keyboard instead. It's super fast and frictionless, which means you can get things done without having to dig through folders or scroll your cursor over your entire desktop or go the Start menu (on a PC) or down to the Dock (on a Mac).

On the Mac, use the free and awesome Quicksilver. On the PC, I like AutoHotKey or Launchy. They all work similarly: you can launch programs and documents with the keyboard, without having to use the mouse or dig through a lot of folders. Quicksilver is by far the best, as it can do so, so much more.

So you need to start writing — with a couple of keystrokes, your trusty writing program launches and you're writing in seconds. You need to look something up or send an email? A few keystrokes away.

Keeping the interface simple like this, without a real need for the Finder or Windows interface, makes things much easier.

Simple Filing

You don't have time to file, to sort all your stuff into a million little folders. You're a busy person! You have bigger and better things to do! Right?

So stop filing. Set up only four folders in your Documents folder:

- 1Inbox: For things you're downloading. I empty this folder daily so it doesn't fill up with junk.

- 2Working: For things you're working on now. Empty it weekly.

- 3Read: For stuff to read. Empty weekly.

- 4Archive: For everything else. When I empty the above three folders, I just dump the files in here. Do I organize it into subfolders and subsubfolders? Heck no! I just dump it all here. Why? Search, and online files. Read on for more.

Search and Online Files

You don't need to organize all your files into folders anymore because of magic called Search. On the Mac, Quicksilver and Spotlight cover this well. On the PC, I recommend Google Desktop. These programs index all your files — including the contents of the files — and put any file at your fingertips in seconds.

I have been using this system for a few years and have never had trouble finding a single document.

Then again, my hard drive doesn't have a lot of documents on it (mostly movies and music and pictures) because I keep most of my documents online. I use Google Docs and Spreadsheets, which means I never file anything. I just search and it's there in half a second.

Keeping all my documents online — even most of my photos are online using Picasa — means they're accessible from any computer, which is important to me as I switch between my iMac and Macbook Air frequently, and sometimes work from other computers. I don't need to sync anything or carry around a USB drive.

I know some people will say, as they always do, that I'm a fool for giving all my data to a company (Google). What if the Internet crashes? What if Google folds? What if they do evil things with all of it?

All good points. I don't see any of that happening soon, and I can always export it all if necessary. I've been using this system for three years without a single problem. In those three years, I would have had to do 17,000 syncs or transfers of files, and my hard drive would have crashed once or twice, losing valuable data if I don't back up.

Tools

Your needs will differ from mine, but I recommend using the simplest programs for the work you need to do.
As a writer, I use TextEdit (on the Mac) or Wordpad (for the PC). I also love, love the program WriteRoom (Mac) or DarkRoom (PC) … it is so beautifully minimalist, and blocks out all distractions as I write.

For to-do lists, I don't like full-featured to-do programs because they're too complicated and invite too much fiddling and distractions. I use Gmail's simple Task app or a simple text file on my desktop computer.

Keep your tools simple. It allows you to focus on what's important: creating.

Going paperless, digitizing

"… in all the things, the supreme excellence is simplicity."
- Henry Wadsworth Longfellow

We are living in a digital world -- an obvious statement, perhaps, but if it's obvious why do we still have so much paperwork in offices?

While at one time I was a paper pusher, several years ago I started re-examining my assumptions, as things became more and more digital. Do I really need this to be in paper form? The answer, in every single case, was "no".

The only reason you can't change something from paper form to digital is that someone -- perhaps you, perhaps a client, perhaps a boss -- is reluctant to change the way things are done. They don't want to figure out a new way to do things, because that can be difficult.

Sure, changing from paper to digital takes some work, but think of the reward: an office that doesn't have mountains of paperwork, that doesn't have huge filing cabinets full of paper files, that doesn't have to spend so much on paper products and waste so many natural resources.

A digital office is a minimalist one in many ways. Information takes up so much less space, for one, which means less storage space is needed and less paper clutter everywhere. There's a lot less work, because you don't have to move things from digital to paper (printing), then physically send it to someone in your office (or worse, outside the office), then move it from paper to digital (data entry), and so on. Also, digital files are searchable, by the computer, while information in paper files takes much longer to find.

So yes, it takes work to go paperless, but the payoff is great, especially for the minimalist.

How to Go Paperless

The main things is to consider every piece of paper, every paper form, every paper note, and ask yourself whether it needs to be paper, and whether it can be made digital or not.

I can almost guarantee you, the answer is no (it doesn't need to be paper) and yes (it can be made digital).

Some examples:

- **Printing things to read**. If you print things out to read, stop. Read it digitally. That was an easy one.

- **Stop keeping paper files**. I used to print things out and file the paper in folders. Now I just keep everything digitally, and have it searchable on my computer.

- **Kill faxes**. If your office still uses it, stop now. It's an outdated technology. Anything that can be faxed can be emailed -- it might mean you need to scan something, but it can be done.

- **Stop sending paper memos and letters**. Also stop circulating documents in paper form. I don't know if people still do this, but email has replaced those uses.

- **Turn all your forms into online forms**. Let people log into a website and fill out the form.

Now you don't need to enter the information from paper forms, and you save tons on printing costs.

- **Invoice digitally**. Lots of great online software to do this.

- **Pay for things digitally**. Stop using checks. Use online banking and Paypal.

- **Stop bills and notices and catalogs and newsletters that come in the mail in paper form**. This takes a phone call for each one.

- **Stop getting paper magazines and newspapers**. They're available online.

- **Stop printing contracts to be signed and then mailed to other parties**. Use an online contract signing service, such as echosign.com -- I've used it and it's fast, easy, and requires no printing or mailing. It's also completely legal.

Again, these are just some examples. Your situation will be different, and the difficulty of going paperless will vary from office to office. You might not be able to eliminate paper, but you can probably reduce it.

Digitizing your physical stuff

You probably have lots of things that are in paper form or in some kind of physical digital format, such as DVDs or CDs. These can all be digitized and stored on the computer, and the physical forms can be trashed or sold or given away.

I've done this with almost everything, from photos to memorabilia to paper records to DVDs and CDs. The result is I have no need for all this clutter, and everything is stored using no physical space.

This also takes a little work, but if you do it a little at a time, it's not hard.

A few notes:

- **Digitize photos**. If you have a lot of old print photos, you can scan them in a little at a time. Or send them to a company that will do them all for you.

- **Take photos of memorabilia**. Do you have little items or papers that have sentimental value? Snap a quick digital photo, and get rid of the item. The memories have been captured.

- **Scan papers**. Again, this can be done a little at a time, or hire a teen-ager (your own or a neighbor or relative) to scan them, or send them to a company that will scan for you.

- **Digitize CDs and DVDs**. There are lots of programs that will rip a CD or DVD, and then you can store all your songs and movies on your computer and have the library accessible via a program such as iTunes. You can do a stack of disks in an afternoon.

Minimalist travel

"I travel light; as light, that is, as a man can travel who will still carry his body around because of its sentimental value."
- Christopher Fry

The minimalist tries to travel as light as possible - a light bag, a light itinerary, and a light attitude.

Many of us have had the nightmare experience of lugging around too much luggage, waiting in the baggage claims area, trying to cram too many activities into each day, and generally being so stressed that we need a vacation when we get home.

Instead, simplify your travel.

My biggest aim is to pack as lightly as possible and to keep my itinerary loose and light. I travel with just a carry-on bag, and don't check luggage, to make things as hassle-free as possible. My carry-on is just a small backpack.

Here's my usual packing list:

- Travel docs (passport, credit card, ID)
- minimal toiletries (deodorant, toothbrush)
- 2 pairs of shorts or jeans (depending on destination)
- 2 T-shirts
- 2 pairs underwear
- swim trunks or hoodie (depending on destination)
- 1 book
- journal and pen

- camera, charger

Anything else I need, I can always get at my destination. I can wash clothes at night. There's no need to take a huge amount of clothing. Obviously, if you're going to a business conference or something like that, your needs will be different, but for vacation, this will usually suffice.

That said, let's look at more ways to travel lightly -- both in what to pack and what to do.

What to Pack

There are lots of different opinions on how to pack light and what items are essential or useful. What follows are a variety of tips, but be aware that there may be contradictory tips here — choose the ones that will work best for you.

- Pack as light as possible. Ask the simple question: "Do I want it or do I need it and if I need it am I will to cart it around?" There is little you really need when you travel.

- Travel with a light backpack. If you are moving between places, backpacks leave your hands free to hold their hands.

- Pack just a few clothes with only a couple complimentary, solid colors — no patterns. Black is a good idea if you need to be able to dress up and be casual.

- Limit yourself to just one pair of shoes, or possibly two if you're a woman.

- Pack only what you can carry on to the flight.

- Put everything you want to bring in a pile and slowly strip away things that aren't necessary.

- Leave the laptop behind, as well as blackberry and any other tech gadget. Being away from the internet's constant flow of data for a few days recharges and relaxes you in ways that you never experience at home.

- Most toiletries can be found easily in your destination country.

- Bring one book, and when you're done, find a book-exchange and trade it for a new one.

- In Asia, sarongs are a traveler's best friend. A sarong works as a towel, a skirt, a makeshift bag, a scarf, a sheet. They're especially good to have if you're traveling low-budget, staying in hostels or guesthouses, which often don't offer towels or even top sheets.

- Mail your purchases home as you go. This reduces what you must carry around with you, what you have to list for customs.

- Don't travel with anything in your pockets except your passport and wallet. You won't have to dig everything out of your pockets every time you go through security. Sitting in the plane is a lot more comfortable as well.

- Photocopies of sections of guidebooks so at the end of a leg of trip the copy goes in the trash.

- Take a photocopy of all your credit cards, passport and any other valuable document you have. Write down the emergency phone number for each credit card beside its photocopy. Leave this with a neighbor or family member along with your itinerary. Should you have your wallet and bags stolen and be only allowed to make one phone call, call this contact person who would be able to cancel your credit cards etc. for you. Alternatively, instead of photocopying your important documents consider scanning them and mailing them to yourself. That way you can always access these documents. Another reader suggested that you should encrypt documents if you email them to yourself.

- Pack only high-tech fabrics, the kind that dry quickly so that you can do a wash in the sink. You can get away with 2 pairs of socks for a 2 week trip by rinsing out the dirty pair at night. High tech fabric means it's dry by the next morning. Cotton will stay soggy for days.

- Tilley makes underwear you can wash in the evening, and it will be dry by morning. You only need two pair, or even one if you are sure of finding somewhere to wash it!

- Tip for quick drying: roll a towel over wet fabric, and squeeze tightly.

- Bring a small amount of foreign currency to cover incidental expenses upon arrival, then change the rest in your destination country, as exchange rates are usually more favorable.

On Planning and Doing

Aside from what to pack, some ideas about what to do when you get to your destination, along with some tips en route to the destination:

46

- Don't overplan your trip. Keep your travel itinerary fluid, so that you can soak up the atmosphere in each place. Leave room for the serendipitous and when plans don't work out, treat it as an opportunity!

- Arrive earlier than you think is necessary — for domestic travel, try to arrive at least 2 hours before flight time; on international, make it three. This reduces the stress of waiting in a long security line as the time of your departure inches ever closer, and those desperate rushes to your boarding area. ▪ Take time for naps. Seriously.

- Smile a lot and talk to the locals.

- Eat, eat, eat and savour the flavors.

- Don't get caught up with sights. Plan some must-dos and leave the rest to chance.

- Wander around at night and stay open to the crazier elements of the culture.

- Get lots of massages.

- Get up early. In hot climates, this will help you avoid the heat of the day; in any climate, it will help you avoid the crowds and get more out of your day at a more leisurely pace. Equally, do the thing you really want to do first, as often plans go awry as the day goes on.

- You shouldn't try and see everything in a given place. In fact, you'll probably have a better time if you focus on meeting great people (instead of going to great places).

Wardrobe and grooming

"When you are content to be simply yourself and don't compare or compete, everybody will respect you."
- Lao Tzu

"Be wary of any enterprise that requires new clothes."
- Henry David Thoreau

Developing a minimalist wardrobe and grooming routine (not to mention grooming products) is a major challenge for most people.

Many people have huge closets and dressers overflowing with clothes -- so many that they can't possibly wear them all, and can't even remember what they have. It's overwhelming and a bit wasteful.

And grooming routines can take an hour for many people, even if they're rushing. They have cabinets and showers and drawers full of grooming products, from hair stuff to makeup to lotions to tweezers and scissors and razors to nail kits to facial products to teeth-care products to soap and shampoo and conditioners and bodywash and facial wash and more.

Now, you might not be as bad as all that, but if you're having trouble getting to minimal, you may want to rethink your needs.

Start with this: you don't need as much as you think you do.

Consider people who live in Third World countries -- many use no grooming products at all, except soap if they're lucky, and have barely any clothing. Now, I'm not suggesting you live like someone in the Third World, but I am saying that what you have is definitely more than you need. It's a matter of finding a balance, so you can live comfortably but not in excess.

Wardrobe

To have a functioning wardrobe without needing too many clothes, it's best to have options that can all go together. Every shirt or top should go with every pants, shorts, or skirt.

The way to do this is to choose a color scheme and a style. For example, I go with plain solid colors, and most of my clothes can all go together -- the colors I use are blue, grey, black, brown, tan and green. I prefer to go without bright colors, but you may be different. Figure out your color scheme.

Stick with a classic style that won't be out of fashion in a few months. Go for high-quality clothes that won't fall apart after a few washes.

Let go of the need to have lots of clothes. Sure, there's a feeling of plenty that comes with having a lot of clothes, and that can be pleasant. But even better is a feeling of having quality over quantity.

Go through your closet. Take everything out, and separate the clothes into two piles: pieces you've worn in the last 6 months, and clothes you haven't. Of course, if it's seasonal, such as a winter coat, give it a 12-month window. Take the pile of clothes you've worn in the last 6 months, and put them back neatly. Donate the rest to charity or give it to a friend who'll use them.

From now on, avoid shopping if possible. Only go clothes or shoe shopping when you absolutely have to -- and even then, consider going to a second-hand shop. When you are tempted to buy something, ALWAYS ask yourself: "Am I going to wear this all the time?"

If the answer is "No" or "I'm not sure", don't buy it.

Grooming

This is a tough area, especially for women. I can't claim to know how to advise women when it comes to grooming, as I absolutely don't understand their needs. My wife, Eva, is far from minimalist, although she's much simpler than many women. She doesn't use hairspray or other products in her hair (she uses a straightener), and she uses minimal makeup (and sometimes none at all). But I don't pretend to understand all the facial and body products she uses.

I'll just describe what I do, then give some suggestions, and allow you to decide what's truly necessary for you.

I've reduced my needs greatly -- not least by shaving my head. I'll admit this isn't for everyone, but for me it has made my life so much simpler. I don't have need for fancy shampoos or conditioners or gels or sprays ... or even combs or brushes, for that matter. All I need for my head is an electric razor, which I apply once a week, and then I forget all about it.

Other than that, I use soap, a toothbrush, toothpaste, a razor (for shaving my beard), shaving cream and deodorant.

I really feel this is all that's necessary. And of course, if you don't shave your face, you need even less. And if you don't mind smelling a little, you don't need deodorant. Soap and toothpaste are pretty mandatory in my book.

What about those who don't shave their heads? I recommend a low-maintenance haircut. Perhaps something short, definitely something that needs minimal styling and brushing and product. Keep it simple.

I also think, if you use facial products or lotions or makeup, you should consider keeping it to a minimum. I won't try to list what that is, but you can probably figure out the simplest possible setup, and get rid of the rest (maybe keeping a few things for special occasions).

Keep it simple, so you can get ready in a flash and not be weighed down by a bunch of clutter and a long routine.

Minimalist food

"Less is more."
  - Ludwig Mies van der Rohe

"Nothing will benefit human health and increase chances for survival of life on Earth as much as the evolution to a vegetarian diet."
- Albert Einstein

Most people would agree that most Americans eat way too much -- and increasingly, much of the rest of the industrialized world.

So for most people, eating less is the answer. Not diet foods or fad diets or health smoothies or liquid cleanses. Just eating less. That's easier said than done, so we'll look at some ways to achieve that.

But minimalism in food goes beyond that. It extends to what you eat, and how you prepare it. You want to eat foods in as natural a state as possible, avoiding processed foods. And you want to prepare them simply, so you don't have to eat fast food or spend all day in the kitchen.

Eat less

If people who are overweight, or on their way to becoming overweight, ate less, many of their health problems would be solved. Sure, eating the right foods and exercising are also important, but excess calories are a fundamental problem for most people.

When you eat too many calories every day, for a long period of time, they're stored as fat. A little fat on your body is necessary, but too much fat causes all kinds of health problems.

So how to eat less? Some ideas:

- Eat until you're almost full. The Okinawans eat until they're 80% full, and they're the healthiest people on earth. Don't wait until you're completely full.

- Eat smaller, lighter meals. Nothing heavy, nothing too big.
- Eat lots of fiber-rich and water-rich foods, such as fruits and veggies and beans. They're filling and healthy.

- Avoid the restaurants that serve huge amounts. Which means most of them. Or only order side dishes or salads if you do go. Or split a huge meal with someone.

- Fast for 18-24 hours, a couple times a week. Sounds counter to most health advice, I know, but read Brad Pilon's Eat Stop Eat book for more info. It works.

Eat clean

While eating less will solve a lot of problems, eating clean is also a good idea. Basically, it's eating food in its natural state, without it being processed.

This doesn't necessarily mean raw food, although raw is good. I'm not advocating a raw diet. I'm advocating a whole food diet, an unprocessed one, often called "clean eating".

So what is clean eating? Here's one definition -- mine:

- Food consumed in its most natural state, or close to it.
- Which means nothing processed.
- Fruits and veggies, of course.
- Nuts, legumes, natural nut butters, nut oils.
- Whole grains, preferably not ground into flour.
- Lean proteins, although I don't eat meat or dairy.

This is my goal, at least. I don't do it 100% of the time. I shoot for about 90%.

This means I have treats, I eat out at restaurants, I can drink beer. Just in moderation.

Cook simply

I highly recommend that you cook for yourself. It will not only save money but save natural resources and it's much healthier.

Eating out at restaurants is convenient, but expensive and usually unhealthy -- even if you make healthy choices, they usually serve way too much, and usually it's not healthy.

So cook for yourself, but do it simply, with simple recipes that don't take a lot of time. Use simple, natural ingredients and some good spices so you can make it taste good without adding a lot of fatty or sugary stuff and without frying.

The best methods for cooking are baking, grilling, stir-frying, and making things like soups.

Some simple recipes to get you started:

- dress up an Amy's Kitchen frozen pizza with some veggies.

  http://www.amys.com/products/category_view.php?prod_category=3

- my favorite healthy breakfast: cook rolled oats and add berries, nuts, other dried or fresh fruits, flaxseed, cinnamon, and a little agave nectar or raw sugar (more healthy breakfasts)

  http://zenhabits.posterous.com/my-favorite-healthy-breakfast

  http://zenhabits.net/2007/09/10-tasty-easy-and-healthy-breakfast-ideas/

- veggie chili

- http://zenhabits.net/2007/02/health-tip-try-eating-vegetarian/

- black bean tacos with lettuce, tomatoes, corn, salsa on corn tortillas

- yogurt, fruit, berries and nuts

- whole grain pita, hummus, olives, tomatoes, spinach

- best soup ever

  http://zenhabits.net/2007/03/recipe-best-soup-ever/

- whole grain pasta, healthy pre-made spaghetti sauce, veggies

- quinoa w/ black beans & corn

  http://allrecipes.com/Recipe/Quinoa-and-Black-Beans/Detail.aspx

Cook more than you need for one meal, so you'll have leftovers for tomorrow.

Minimalist kitchen setup

Keep your kitchen minimalist as well. Only keep as many dishes and silverware and pots and pans as you need. A couple of good, sharp knives and a cutting board. That's pretty much all you need.

Don't have single-use kitchen tools and gadgets -- they waste space. Things such as a juice maker, waffle iron, ice cream scooper, and on and on. You will barely use them and they're not needed.

Veganism

You don't need to be a vegan or vegetarian to be a minimalist, and I'm not going to try to convert you here. But I think the two philosophies mesh very well, because they try to use as few resources as possible. A vegan, in a very minimalist way, will only eat what's necessary. And as meat and dairy and eggs aren't necessary for healthy living (they're luxuries), a vegan will do without them, especially as a vegan doesn't see them as ethical.

Becoming vegetarian or vegan doesn't have to be difficult, nor does it have to be instantaneous. Like any of the changes in this book, you do them slowly, gradually, over time. That's sustainable, and it's manageable. Gradually eat more vegetarian meals, dropping one kind of meat or animal product at a time. You'll get used to it.

Being a vegan is actually just as liberating as being a minimalist, because you realize that before becoming vegan, you were tied to meat and other animal products almost involuntarily, because of advertising and a culture of excess.

Minimalist fitness

"People love chopping wood. In this activity one immediately sees results."
- Albert Einstein

We've covered eating healthier, but what about exercise? This is another tough area for a lot of people, because many people either hate exercise or put it off for various reasons.

But getting fit doesn't have to be difficult or complicated. What's the minimal amount of exercise you need to get fit? What kind of exercise do you need to do, and what kind of equipment do you need?

Minimalist fitness focuses on working out less than others would have you do, with less equipment. Two common barriers for people who want to exercise and get in shape are a lack of time and money needed for fitness.

Less time

Exercise doesn't need to take an hour or two each day -- you can get by on an hour or two a week if you do it right.

In fact, if you're just starting out in exercise, I suggest you start small, and start slowly. Just start walking, if you've been inactive, for 15-20 minutes a few times a week. If you've been active, 20 minutes a day, 5 days a week would be great. Eventually getting up to 30 minutes is even better, but you can get a great workout in just 20 minutes.

Who doesn't have 15-20 minutes to save their lives? Do it in the morning, after you wake up, at lunch, or right after work on the way home.

If you've been active for a few months, you can get a great workout by doing intervals (walk-run, or jog-run, or biking slow then fast, or swimming), or by doing some of the bodyweight workouts below.

The key is to get active, most days of the week (4-5 is best). Get outside, do something fun. Play basketball, go skating, surf, run and jump with your kids, play soccer or rugby, climb or hike or paddle.

If you go longer than 20-30 minutes, because you're having fun, that's OK, but it's not necessary.

Minimal equipment

It takes no equipment to get a great workout and get in shape, and with one or two pieces of simple equipment, you can turn that great workout into a fantastic one.

And with little or no equipment required for a fantastic workout, you can do it at home, or wherever you are. It's hard not to find time for this type of workout — you can even do it while watching TV!

Using just your bodyweight, you can do a large number of challenging exercises. I designed a workout that I do when I can't make it to the gym, for example, and I can testify that it's incredibly challenging.

If you add just one or two pieces of equipment: a dumbbell, a kettlebell, a jump rope, a medicine ball, or a chinup bar, for example, you can increase the challenge even more.

Bodyweight workouts are great because there are no gym fees or need to buy expensive equipment, you can do the workout anywhere, anytime, most exercises involve many muscles working in coordination, resulting in great overall fitness and strength, and for people who are just starting with strength training, bodyweight is often more than enough to begin with. And it gives you a good foundation of strength you can build on later.

I suggest starting with bodyweight exercises, and then slowly transitioning to a combination of bodyweight and weight training to get a good balance. And even if you're doing a complete weight training program, you can always use bodyweight exercises anytime you can't make it to the gym.

A sample bodyweight workout: a circuit of pullups, pushups, jump squats, bicycle crunches, jumping lunges, burpees, hanging knee raises, diamond pushups, planks, chinups. This is by no means the only way to do it -- there are tons of other bodyweight exercises you can choose from, and you should mix it up with a variety of cardio exercises as well.

Get outside and get active. Walk or run or bike. Mix in some dumbbells, barbells, kettlebells, jump rope, martial arts. As you get better, make your workouts short but intense. Also try Crossfit to really challenge yourself with a minimalist workout. http://crossfit.com/

Minimalist finances

"Too many people spend money they haven' t earned, to buy things they don' t want, to impress people they don' t like."
    -   **Will Rogers**

"He looks the whole world in the face for he owes not any man."
- Henry Wadsworth Longfellow

Finances are one of the most complicated things in many people's lives ... and yet, they don't have to be.
With a little effort, you can simplify your financial life and end the money headaches most people face.

Here's how to simplify your financial life:

1. **End consumerism**.

   This is the first and most important step. Too often we get into the mindset of buying, of attaining more, of shopping for pleasure or stress relief or finding self-worth, of impulse buys. This is a mindset that comes from years of exposure to advertising, and it's hard to stop. Start by becoming more conscious of it, and by telling yourself that you will no longer find pleasure in buying and having material things. When you find yourself with an urge to buy, stop, and breathe. Put the item on a 30-day list and don't buy it until 30 days after you put it on the list -- usually the impulse will dissipate. Give thought to every purchase and ask yourself, "Is this really, really necessary? Can I live without it?" Try to live only with what's necessary, and get happiness from doing things, from spending time with people, from creating ... rather than from material goods and spending.

2. Save up an emergency fund.

Before you can find financial peace of mind, you need an emergency fund, otherwise you're always going to be living on the edge, from paycheck to paycheck. Every unexpected expense that comes up will derail everything I recommend below, if you have no emergency fund. This point has been driven home many times on this site, so I won't belabor it. But start here. Save up at least $500 by putting $50-100 per paycheck towards this fund, and gradually build up to $1000 or more.

To do this, cut out unnecessary expenses. Look closely at your spending, including regular payments you might have forgotten about, and see what can be cut. There's always something: magazine subscriptions, monthly payments for services you don't really need (including online services), buying books when you could use the library, cable TV, a bigger car than you really need, gourmet coffee when you can make your own at home, a bigger home than you need, storage space when you could just sell your stuff, clothes and shoes when you already have plenty, gadgets and computer purchases you don't really need, going out to lots of restaurants or bars or clubs or other expensive entertainment when you could stay home or do fun things without spending much. Put all money you cut out into your emergency fund until it gets to at least $500.

3. Get out of debt.

This is important -- otherwise, minimalist finances will be difficult to achieve. Debt payments are not essential

-- you shouldn't have them in the first place. But until you pay them off, they'll be headaches.

After you've saved at least $500 for your emergency fund, put most of your extra income towards debt payment, one debt at a time, until you're all paid up. Maybe put a little each paycheck towards your emergency fund. This step will take the longest, but it's well worth it. And you can do the other stuff on this list immediately, without having to complete this step first.

4. Use cash, not credit.

I'm a big fan of cash, and a big credit card hater. Credit card bills are a blight on most people's finances -- they make it too easy to spend money you don't have, and then you end up paying tons in interest and fees. Sure, it's possible to use them responsibly, but in most cases, it's not necessary and it's an unnecessary temptation. Ditch the credit cards and use cash and (sometimes) Visa or Mastercard debit cards -- these are better as they only allow you to spend money you already have and not get into debt.

Cash is great because you can withdraw a pre-determined amount each month, and you always know how much you have left. With credit cards, it's easy to spend more than you have budgeted because to stay within a budget you'll have to constantly track your expenses. No need to track expenses with cash -- you can see you only have a little left. Try the envelope system for cash -- put designated amounts of cash into separate envelopes for groceries, gas and other spending.

5. Automate finances.

I don't like to worry about paying bills, so I've made my finances automagical. Basically, I have all my income automatically deposited in my checking account, and I've set up automatic payment for all bills. Some are done by automatic deduction, when possible, and others are done by using the online bill-paying system of my bank, set to recurring monthly payments. Other bills I've paid in big chunks, 6 months to a year at a time -- my rent, for example -- when I received large payments (such as tax returns or bonuses). I also make savings transfers automatic, and when I was in debt, those payments were automatic as well.

It helps to have a sizable emergency fund so you can make payments like this and not worry about whether there's enough in your account for all of your automatic bill payments. I've actually split my emergency fund into two: most is in an online savings account, and the rest is in my checking, so I always have a comfortable cushion in my checking account.

It takes a little while to get automated finances just right, but you can start today by setting up automatic deposits and deductions and bill payments. It's nice, because your finances also become paperless.

I recommend putting a reminder in your calendar to check on your bank accounts once a week, just for peace of mind. Otherwise, you can now forget about finances.

6. Don't buy unless you need it and have the money.

This is such an old and commonsense piece of advice that it's embarrassing to put it here, but it's important, because once you've done all of the above, you're debt-free with a good emergency fund and automatic finances ... but what about purchases from now on? Should I buy a bike if I want to commute by bike? Should I buy new furniture? The answer is two-fold: 1) don't buy it unless you really need it; and 2) don't buy it unless you have the money already. Not "if you have the money next month or next week", but only if you have the money in hand. It's as simple as that.

Stay out of debt as much as possible. The last car I bought was used, and I was able to pay cash for it (with a trade-in). I hope to buy my first house completely with cash, or at least mostly.

Don't buy it unless you need it, and only if you have the money. If you follow these two rules, you'll never have to worry about finances again.

Finding simplicity with kids

"You can learn many things from children. How much patience you have, for instance."
    -   **Franklin P. Jones**

"Your children need your presence more than your presents."
    -   **Jesse Jackson**

Any parent knows that kids create clutter like nobody's business. It's enough to drive a minimalist such as myself crazy -- especially as I have six kids. Still, with a little diligence, and a little bit of Zen detachment, it's possible to have a simple, (relatively) uncluttered home as well as peace of mind.

Let me first state the obvious: any life that includes children is going to be complicated, at least to some degree. You'll never get an absolute minimalist lifestyle with kids, and I've learned to accept that. While my minimalist inner self would like to live without a car, a cell phone, or a large house, my kids preclude those things from happening.

However, I have found ways to simplify my house, including the kids' rooms. Sure, the house still gets messy — especially their rooms. But it's not as bad as it once was, and it's at a manageable level.

Attitudes

It's important to start with the right attitudes -- both for you, and your kids. All the decluttering in the world won't matter unless you address this first.

First, you must realize that kids are messy, and that they don't care about clutter like you do. You'll never change this -- although some kids are naturally neater than most. You must start by accepting this, and not trying to force your system on them. It will only end in frustration.

Better is to take a more relaxed approach. Let kids be kids, but find ways to educate them about material goods, and find ways to contain their clutter. Do the decluttering for them -- but let them help and be a part of it -- and find a compromise you can all live with. Being relaxed about it will keep your sanity.

Next, you might try to talk to the kids, get them to take the right attitude about possessions. They might not understand at first, but as you lead by example and educate them, they'll eventually come to share in many of your values about material goods and clutter, even if they aren't good at being minimal or organized or neat. At the very least, they'll be more aware of it when they go out and become adults, and then they can decide what to do from there.

Kids clutter

Here are my tips for simplifying clutter with kids:

- **Identify the important**. The first step in decluttering is identifying which toys and other possessions are truly important to the kids. What do they play with, what do they love? Then get rid of as much of the rest as possible, keeping only those they use and love.

- **Massively purge**. In the beginning, if you have a lot of kid clutter, you'll want to go through a massive purge. The way to do this is to block off a day to go through their rooms. Do one area at a time: a drawer, a section of the closet, a shelf. Take everything out of that area, put it in a pile. From that pile, take only the really important stuff (See Tip 1). Get rid of the rest. Donate it to charity if it's still good. Get some boxes and put all the stuff to donate in there, and when they're full, load them up in your car to donate on your next trip. Then put back the important stuff, and tackle the next area. If you do this quickly, you can do a room in a couple of hours.

- **Leave space**. When you put the important stuff back, don't try to fill up each drawer, shelf or closet area. Allow there to be some space around the objects. It's much nicer looking, and it leaves room for a couple of extra items later if necessary.

- **Contain**. The key for us has been to contain the kid clutter. We only let them keep their stuff in their rooms. The living room, kitchen and dining room are for household stuff only. We do have a play area for the two toddlers, and their stuff gets spread throughout the house, but still, we try to contain the kid stuff to certain areas only. This leaves our living area very simple and minimal.

- **Bins**. These are the best type of containers for kids stuff, in general. Bins or baskets. The key is to make it easy for the kids (or you) to toss their stuff into the bins, making cleanup simple. Label each bin, if possible, with the type of stuff that goes there (blocks, stuffed animals, Legos, instruments of destruction). If your child can't read, use picture labels.

- **Cubbies**. We have a small plastic 3drawer organizer (we call them "cubbies") for each child. They don't take up much room in the closets, and it allows them to have a place to put their little odds and ends that would otherwise be all over the place.

- **A home for everything**. We haven't actually completely succeeded at this, but we try to teach the kids that everything they own has a "home". This means that if they're going to put away a toy, they should know where its home is, and put it there. If they don't know where the home is, they need to find a home for it, and put it there from now on. Actually, this is a useful concept for adults, too, and it's one that I've mastered and found very useful. Our kids understand this idea (at least, the four older ones do), but sometimes they forget. Still, it helps keep things organized.

- **Organize like with like**. Try to keep similar things organized together. So, one bin for stuffed animals, another for sports stuff. This makes it easier to remember. Same thing with clothes: underwear and socks together, shirts, shorts, pants, etc. All video game stuff in one place.

- **One place for school papers**. Similarly, you should have one place to keep all incoming school papers. We have an inbox for all incoming papers in our house, but we also keep a folder to store school papers, so we never have to search for them. Also, when we get a school calendar or a notification of some school event, we enter it in our Google Calendar, so we never forget when stuff is.

- **Teach them to clean**. All our kids know how to clean up after themselves, including our 3-year-old. So, instead of us continually stressing out about the messes, we just ask them to clean up now and then. Sure, things will get messy again soon.

But at least the kids are doing the work cleaning up, not us. :)

- **Allow them to mess**. Kids are not perfect. They will inevitably make a mess. You have to allow them to do this. Then, when they're done, ask them to clean it up. No harm, no foul.

- **Purge at Christmas, birthdays**. On these two occasions, new stuff comes into their lives en masse. If you just add this new stuff to their old stuff, you will have a huge mess. Instead, we ask them to put all their gifts in one place. Then, a day or two after Christmas or their birthday, we go through their closets and bins and ask them what they want to get rid of so they can make room for the new stuff.

- **Do regular decluttering**. Every month or two, you'll need to declutter their stuff again. Do it at least quarterly. You could put a reminder in your calendar, or just look at their rooms every now and then, and if it looks way too cluttered, schedule some time to do some purging.

- **Less is more**. Teach the kids that they don't need to have huge piles of stuff to be happy. They can't possibly play with everything anyway — there aren't enough hours in the day. With less stuff, they can find things more easily, they can see what there is to play with, and they can own better quality stuff (see next tip).

- **Go for quality**. Instead of getting them a huge pile of cheap junk, go for quality toys or possessions that will last long. Wood is better than plastic, for example. The classic toys are often the best. It's best to spend your money on a couple of great things than a whole bunch of cheap things that will break and be relegated to the junk pile in no time.

- **Buy less**. Drastically reduce the amount of stuff you buy for your kids. It's difficult to resist them when they really want something at a store, I know, but you aren't doing them any favors by caving in. Don't deprive them completely, but also don't spoil them with stuff. On Christmas, for example, just get them a few great things rather than a whole bunch of stuff.

- **Clean as you go**. I've learned to clean up messes as I go (or ask the kids to clean up their mess), so that the house is never a wreck.

- **Clean before bed**. I also do a quick clean-up right before I go to bed, getting any little things the little ones forgot to put away. It makes my mornings much more pleasant.

- **30-minute cleanups**. On Saturdays, do a "30-minute cleanup". This means that every child (over 5 years old probably) has a chore, and the whole family (including parents) pitch in to clean up the house. Set a timer, and see if you can do it all in 30 minutes. That's much easier for our family to accomplish, as we have six people (including two adults and a teenager) pitching in to finish quickly. This gives us a clean house and the rest of the day to have fun.

- **Prep time**. This isn't so much to do with clutter as with general simplifying your life with kids. It helps to have prep time each evening and morning to prepare the kids' lunches, clothes, or whatever is needed for whatever we're doing that day. This means we get the soccer gear and drinks and snacks ready on soccer days, or whatever gear is necessary for the activities of the day. It saves a rush when you are trying to get out the door, and saves you from forgetting stuff later.

Dealing with non-minimalist loved ones

"You must be the change you want to see in the world."
- **Gandhi**

One of the biggest challenges for anyone wanting to live a minimalist life is not internal but external — their loved ones aren't on board the minimalist train. How do you deal with that? What's the simple solution?

There isn't one.

Dealing with others who might be hoarders, clutter-bugs, just plain messy, or maybe just regular people who don't care about minimalism … it's not easy. It's so much easier to live alone and not have to worry about the living habits and preferences of others, but many of us don't have that "luxury" (although there are a few benefits of living with those who love you).

Here are some strategies that have worked for me. Your mileage will definitely vary.

1. **Focus on yourself**. While your spouse or partner or children may not want to declutter their lives or live without consumerism, you can, at least in the areas you control. You can stop buying. You can get rid of things you personally own that you don't need. You can find joy in doing rather than owning or buying. You can reduce what you do, what you consume, what you eat, and so on. These you control, and they should be your first focus.

2. **Lead by example**. You must remember that others are people with their own beliefs and way of living —

77

which you cannot control. However, you can influence them. And one of the best ways of influencing others is by example. Live a life of minimalism, and show how wonderful it can be. Show how easy — and actually fun — it can be to declutter. Show how happy you are. Share it all with those around you. Do it without trying to push it on them, because they will react negatively to being forced or nagged into doing anything.

3. **Educate**. Often people are against change because they don't know enough about it. Combat this ignorance with non-pushy education. Talk with your loved ones about what you're doing and why. Show them examples of people who inspire you. Send them links to mnmlism.com, Zen Habits and other blogs and magazines you enjoy — not as a hint, but as a way to share things you're excited about. Over time, they'll start to understand, and maybe even join you.

4. **Ask for help**. Your loved ones, most likely, care about you. They want you to be happy — but want to be happy themselves. Enlist your loved ones' desire to make you happy … ask them for help. Say, "I need your help in getting to the minimalist life I want. Do you think you can help me?" Of course, if you've educated them, they already know what you want, but most people would love to help you if they can. Don't ask them to change, but ask if they can help you declutter, or keep a certain area uncluttered, or figure out a solution to a problem you're facing.

5. **Set boundaries**. If you can't get a loved one on board, it helps to set boundaries. For kids, ask them to keep their clutter to their rooms. Give them that personal space, and don't bug them about it. For adults, you might designate certain rooms or areas as yours and others as theirs. I've known some people who've split

rooms or entire homes in half — one side is uncluttered, and the other was … not.

6. **Find compromises**. Living with other people means finding ways of living that work for everyone. That might mean you need to give a little, if you want to ask them to give a little in return. Be willing to accept a less-than-perfect solution, if the solution will work for everyone.

7. **Find acceptance**. In the end, you might not win over the people who live with you — and you can either be frustrated or angry with that, or you can accept it. The second option is preferred, as you'll have more peace of mind. It's not easy, and will require you letting go of certain expectations, letting go of a need to control, and learning to love someone for who they are, not who you want them to be. But in the end, the effort will be worth it.

Minimalism is the end of organizing

"The ability to simplify means to eliminate the unnecessary so that the necessary may speak."
- Hans Hofmann

The rise of clutter has given birth to a whole industry: organizing.

We now have legions of professional organizers, whole companies that sell organizing products such as closet organizers, magazines and blogs on how to get yourself organized, and of course, the hand-held notebooks we call organizers — and their digital equivalent, PDAs and mobile devices.

And while I have nothing against professional organizers — they help people to find peace in lives of chaos — I don't think they're necessary ... if you adopt minimalism.

Organizing is only necessary when you have too many things to easily find what you're looking for.

Think about it: when we organize a collection of books, it's because when they're not organized, we can't find the books we want. But if we had, say, five books, we wouldn't need to organize.

The same applies to anything that needs to be organized:

- Closets that have a minimal amount of things don't need to be organized.

- Tasks only need a complicated system or productivity apps for organizing if you have a lot to do. Focus on only doing a few important things, and you barely even need a list.

- Finances only need organizing if they're complicated. I'll write about minimalist finances later.

- Files only need to be organized if you can't let go of this need to organize them. With search so powerful these days, you can find things with a few keystrokes.

There are lots of other things that need to be organized, if they're not kept as simple as possible. I'm sure you can think of a few yourself. Consider making them as minimalist as possible, and the organizing will fade away.

Step lightly upon this world: on sustainability

"Walk lightly in the spring; Mother Earth is pregnant."
- Native American (Kiowa) proverb

There's a lot we can learn from traditional cultures such as the Native Americans. Including the idea of walking lightly upon this earth.

It's something we've forgotten in hundreds of years of striving to achieve more, to produce more, to build bigger and better things.

We have forgotten to walk lightly, and instead mine the earth of its natural resources, clearcut forests, pollute rivers and lakes and oceans, alter the landscape to fit our needs, make the air dirty and the rain acidic and the ozone holed.

This isn't news. We're all aware of the problems, but the solutions are less obvious.

Do I buy greener products? Do I buy a greener car? Do I recycle all the stuff I use?

Well, sure. You can do all of those things, and they are useful. But even better: live a life of less, and walk lighter. A life of less means you consume less, use fewer natural resources, pollute less, own less stuff, contribute less to greenhouse emissions.

Minimalism, the philosophy of a life of less, is more sustainable because it uses less, and thus recycling isn't as necessary (though it's still important). It's not sustainable to continue to consume huge amounts of products (no matter how green they are) or use natural resources (no matter how organic).

There's a lot to write about here, and I'll write more later, but a few brief examples:

- **Buy less stuff**. Buying a lot of products is at the heart of this. Read more:

  Why less stuff is better
  http://mnmlist.com/why-less-stuff-is-better/

  Consumerism vs. minimalism
  http://mnmlist.com/consumerism-vs-minimalism/

  Rethinking necessities
  http://mnmlist.com/rethinking-necessities/

- **Eat less**. Americans as a group eat way too much. It's not just about the huge amounts of natural resources that go into producing all of that food, although that's huge (read about the rainforests being clearcut to make grazing room for McDonald's beef cows, for example). It's also about the huge wasteful restaurants, from McDonald's to Chilis to Lone Star, serving ridiculous amounts of fat and salt and sugar laden food (and throwing much of it away), when we could simply eat at home. It's about all the packaging that goes into all our frozen and processed food. It's about the health problems that arise from eating so much unhealthy food, and the wasted resources that go into caring for all our diseased people, too fat from all the eating.

- **Eat less meat**. Meat is not sustainable. Most of the crops we grow go to feeding animals raised for food or dairy or eggs. If we stopped eating so much meat, we would use fewer resources and could feed more people.

- **Use less packaging**. It's insane how much packaging is used in all the products we buy. Unfortunately, there isn't much choice when you want to buy something. Choose products with less packaging when you do have a choice. I think the public demanding less packaging will get manufacturers to change this wasteful practice.

- **Drive less**. Walk more. Start cycling. Use mass transit. Carpool. Consolidate trips. Stay home sometimes.

- **Have a smaller house**. Have less stuff, and you need less space. Big houses are wasteful, not only in the resources they take to build, but in cooling and heating and maintaining.

Again, just a few examples. It's really a mindset, not a laundry list of things to do.

FAQs

"Simplicity, simplicity, simplicity! I say let your affairs be as one, two, three and to a hundred or a thousand... We are happy in proportion to the things we can do without."
- Henry David Thoreau

Some frequently asked questions (FAQs) about minimalism and living the minimalist life, for those new to the concept.

Q: Why be a minimalist?

A: It's a way to escape the excesses of the world around us — the excesses of consumerism, material possessions, clutter, having too much to do, too much debt, too many distractions, too much noise. But too little meaning. Minimalism is a way of eschewing the non-essential in order to focus on what's truly important, what gives our lives meaning, what gives us joy and value.

Q: Isn't minimalism boring or too sparse, with nothing in your life?

A: This is a misconception about minimalism — that it's necessarily monk-like, empty, boring, sterile. Not at all. Well, it can be, if you go in that direction, but I don't advocate that flavor of minimalism. Instead, we are clearing away all but the most essential things — to make room for that which gives us the most joy. Clear away the distractions so we can create something incredible. Clear away all the obligations so we can spend time with loved ones. Clear away the noise so we can concentrate on inner peace, on spirituality (if we wish), on our thinking. As a result, there is more happiness, peace, and joy, because we've made room for these things.

Q: What is minimalist living?

A: It's simply getting rid of things you do not use or need, leaving an uncluttered, simple environment and an uncluttered, simple life. It's living without an obsession with material things or an obsession with doing everything and doing too much. It's using simple tools, having a simple wardrobe, carrying little and living lightly.

Q: What are the benefits of minimalism?

A: There are many. It's lower in stress. It's less expensive and less debt. It's less cleaning and maintaining. It's more enjoyable. There's more room for creating, for loved ones, for peace, for doing the things that give you joy. There's more time for getting healthy. It's more sustainable. It's easier to organize. These are only the start.

Q: What does the schedule of a minimalist look like?

A: There's no single answer to this question, but a minimalist would probably focus on doing less, on having a less cluttered schedule, but what's on his or her schedule would be important. A minimalist might not actually keep a schedule or calendar, at one extreme, if he didn't have much to do each day — he might instead live and work moment-by-moment, or just decide each morning to focus on one or two important things.

A minimalist would also save a lot of time because of having less clutter and fewer possessions. That means less time cleaning and maintaining, and less time searching for things. A minimalist who clears away distractions and single-tasks would also waste less time with those distractions and in switching back and forth between tasks (multi-tasking).

In general, all this results in more time for relaxing, for hobbies, for creating, for doing fun things. See http://zenhabits.net/2007/02/how-not-to-multitask-work-simpler-and/

Q: What rules do I need to follow to become minimalist?

A: There are no set rules. There's no one way. What I suggest for living minimally isn't what someone else would recommend, nor is it how you would live your minimalist life. In general, however, you want to live simply without too many unnecessary possessions, distractions, clutter, or waste. You want to live frugally, debt-free, sustainably, naturally.

Q: Do you need to be vegan or vegetarian to be minimalist?

A: No. While I believe the vegan/vegetarian lifestyle is consistent with minimalism, you can eat simply as an omnivore as well. Again, there's no one way. A minimalist would try to eat naturally, without too much processing, and not eat too much food (such as the ridiculous portions at most restaurants these days).

Q: Aren't you being contradictory by claiming to be a minimalist and owning a Mac, or a house, or having six kids?

A: Again, there's no one way. Everyone must find his own path, and mine is different than what someone else would consider minimalist. Also, I have never claimed to be perfect — I'm striving for minimalism, but I always have room for improvement. I have things that are inconsistent with minimalism, or at least by the definition of others. I'm working on it.

I should say a word or two about having six kids and minimalism. Having six children is inconsistent with my message of simplifying, frugality, downsizing, being green. I don't have a defense ... but I do have an explanation for the inconsistency. I had my kids before (and during) my change in philosophy. In fact, my philosophy is evolving even now, so I can't claim to have believed in the things I believe in now, for a very long time. Many things I believe in are only recent developments.

As an example — only recently, I made the decision to transition back into veganism (I was vegan once, but have been lacto-ovo veggie for over a year). But I own a pair of leather sandals — do I throw them out? Wouldn't that be wasteful? Is it better to be wasteful but consistent with my beliefs? It's hard to say.

However, I have decided it would be most unethical for me to throw out my children, just because I now believe in downsizing. As a result of my simplifying, I am able to enjoy my time with my children, and I have to admit, they are the best thing to happen to me. I don't regret having them one bit, even if they are inconsistent with my philosophy of downsizing.

On the good side, I believe that even with six kids, being vegan, buying less stuff, being energy conscious, owning only one car and rarely driving it, walking more for transportation .... I actually use fewer resources than the average person in developed countries (and far less than the avg American) — this is according to online carbon footprint calculators. It's not a justification for having six kids, but just a note that things aren't as bad as they could be.

Other resources

**"It looks like you can write a minimalist piece without much bleeding. And you can. But not a good one."
- David Foster Wallace**

Some of my favorite minimalist blogs and tumblelogs:

- mnmlist.com

- ZenHabits.net

- Minima http://minima.al3x.net/

- Becoming Minimalist
  http://www.becomingminimalist.com/

- Minimal Mac http://minimalmac.com/

- The Minimalist http://theminimalist.net/

- Simple. Organized. Life.
  http://simpleorganizedlife.com/

- On Simplicity http://www.onsimplicity.net/

- Urban Minimalist Lifestyle
  http://urbanminimalistlife.blogspot.com/

- The Minimal List http://www.theminimallist.com/

- Unclutterer http://unclutterer.com/

Good articles on minimalism:

- Why the minimalist lifestyle appeals to me (blissful buzz) http://blissfullydomestic.com/2008/why-the-minimal

- Paul Graham: Stuff http://www.paulgraham.com/stuff.html

- The Minimalist Manifesto http://theminimalist.net/the-minimalist-manifesto/

- The Suckless manifest http://suckless.org/manifest/

- Why the minimalist lifestyle appeals to me (being frugal) http://beingfrugal.net/2007/09/25/why-the-minimalist-lifestyle-appeals-to-me/

- 5 ways to become a minimalist today http://lifeexcursion.com/index.php/5-simple-ways-to-become-a-minimalist-today/

- Practical minimalism guide: a functional house http://papabusy.com/practical-minimalism-guide-functional-house/

- How to live with just 100 things http://papabusy.com/practical-minimalism-guide-functional-house/

- Why work? http://www.whywork.org/

- Freeganism http://en.wikipedia.org/wiki/Freeganism

On sustainability:

- The Green Audacity of Lifestyle Minimalism
  http://www.jetsongreen.com/2008/03/the-green-audac.html

- How to Maintain a Sustainable Minimalist Lifestyle
  http://www.ehow.com/how_4665836_maintain-sustainable-minimalist-lifestyle.html

- No Impact Man   http://noimpactman.typepad.com/

- Carfree Family http://carfreefamily.blogspot.com/

On frugality:

- Get Rich Slowly
  http://www.getrichslowly.org/blog/

- The Simple Dollar
  http://www.thesimpledollar.com/

- Wise Bread http://www.wisebread.com/

On traveling light:

- One bag http://www.onebag.com/

- Tim Ferriss: How to travel the world with 10 lbs or less
  http://www.fourhourworkweek.com/blog/2007/07/11/how-to-travel-the-world-with-10-pounds-or-less-plus-how-to-negotiate-convertibles-and-luxury-treehouses/

Recommended books:

- Zen to Done - The Ultimate Simple Productivity System by Leo Babauta

  http://www.amazon.com/Zen-Done-Ultimate-Simple-Productivity/dp/1438258488/ref=sr_1_1?ie=UTF8&s=books&qid=1255298910&sr=8-1

- Power of Less, The: The Fine Art of Limiting Yourself to the Essential…in Business and in Life by Leo Babauta

- Your Money or Your Life by Joe Dominguez and Vicki Robin

- Simplify Your Life by Elaine St. James

- Radical Simplicity by Jim Merkel

Acknowledgements

Books are not created in a vacuum, and all the people who help make a book a reality cannot be named. I'd have to go back to thanking everyone from my college professors to my mother (btw, thanks mom!).

As I can't be complete, I'll risk offending with a few words of thanks:

- My wife Eva, who as always gave me the time and freedom to write by taking care of everything else and shielding me from the worries of the world.

- My kids, who inspire me to be better.

- Fellow bloggers such as J.D. Roth of Get Rich Slowly, the folks at Lifehacker.com, Darren of Problogger, Brian of Copyblogger, Mary of Goodlife Zen, Glen of LifeDev, Erin of Unclutterer, Gretchen of The Happiness Project, Cyan and Collis of Freelanceswitch, and so many other blogging friends who have inspired, encouraged and supported me along the way.

- Minimalist bloggers around the world, from Becoming Minimalist, Alex Payne, David of The Good Human, Sara of OnSimplicity, and many more, who have also inspired me.

- All my family, who are just awesome.

Bonus Articles:

A Minimalist's Guide to Using Twitter Simply, Productively, and Funly

This morning after our hill run my sister asked me about Twitter: "What's Twitter all about? I don't get it?"

Neither did I at first — I resisted using Twitter for more than a year because it seemed like just another distraction, just another way to waste time and have noisy chatter going on in front of you.

But I decided to see what the fuss was all about, and did my Great Twitter Experiment. See http://zenhabits.net/2008/08/the-great-twitter-experiment/ To my surprise, Twitter was actually fun, interesting, and useful — if used correctly.

I've also found that Twitter isn't something you can explain, and it's not something you can understand until you've used it for at least a few days. You have to use it to get it.

I think that's because Twitter can be so many things to so many people. One person might use it as a marketing tool, another to stay in touch with friends, another to collaborate with co-workers, and still others to stay informed about their favorite bloggers, websites, the latest gossip, reading, news and more.

Today we'll look at some different ways you can use Twitter without spending too much time doing it.

A Minimalist Approach

When I first signed up for Twitter a few months ago, I followed a bunch of people I knew and was instantly fed with a stream of new "tweets" from all the people I was following. I read through all the tweets, but the stream just kept coming.

I'd wake up in the morning and try to read through all the tweets, or at least scan them. Then I'd try to keep up periodically throughout the day. It was stressful.

Then I learned the secret of Twitter: don't try to keep up.

Twitter is like a river … you can step into it at any point and feel the water, bathe in it, frolic if you like … and then get out. And go back in at any time, at any point. But, you don't have to try to consume the entire river — it's impossible and frankly a waste of time in my eyes.

So that's how I approach Twitter these days: I'll just jump into the stream of incoming tweets and see what people are saying. I can ignore them or follow their links or reply if I want. Then I get out of the stream. I don't try to read everything I missed, and if I miss a lot of stuff, I'm OK with that.

I've actually used this approach I learned from with other things, such as email, Facebook, RSS, news and other information. I don't have to consume it all, but I can jump into the river anytime I like and read, reply if I like, and get back out. So what if I miss a ton of blog posts, news stories, and emails? Will my life fall apart?

The answer turns out to be no.

Simple Ways to Use Twitter

If you follow this minimalist approach, you don't have to spend a lot of time using Twitter to get a lot out of it, no matter what your goals are.

Here are some guidelines and ideas for using Twitter that I've found to be useful:

98

- **Don't follow a lot of people**. Some people follow thousands of people. Their incoming stream must be incredible — I'm sure they don't even try to keep up with everything. Others might be even more minimalist than I am: they follow a dozen people or less. But then what's interesting about that? You're not getting very much out of Twitter if you only follow a few people. Your needs will be different than mine, but I've found that following a few dozen to a hundred people is ideal if you're trying to keep things simple but still get a lot out of Twitter. I think I'm following about 60 right now. I add people now and then but also drop others if they tweet too often and I don't get anything out of their tweets.

- **Don't tweet too much**. Some people are constantly tweeting. Personally, I don't like to read that many every hour, so if they're filling up my stream of incoming tweets, they're wasting my time. I've found that once a day or a few times a day or even 10 times a day at the most is ideal for me — your usage will vary. But if you do it too much, you have to be using Twitter a lot, and to me that's too much of a distraction and time drain. So I go on a few times a day (at most) and tweet only when I feel I have something interesting to say or ask.

- **Don't be on Twitter all the time**. Some people have it open all the time — and that's fine if it works for you. Personally, I've found that if Twitter is open (or if Twitterific, my desktop Twitter program, is open) all the time, I have a hard time focusing on other work. So like I said, I close it most of the time and open it a few times a day to see what's going on. Mainly when I want to take a break. I only open it for a few minutes at most.

- **Make announcements**. I like to announce things on Twitter — it's more effective than announcing things through email and less obtrusive than doing an entire post on my blog.

- **Ask questions**. Sometimes I'll need a solution or some ideas for something, and I'll ask the question on Twitter — and immediately get a dozen great replies. Thank you Twitterers! One time I couldn't order a notebook (Muji Chronotebook) online so I asked if anyone lived near a Muji store, in New York for instance — and one Twitterer actually went to the store and bought it for me, and mailed it to me! Btw, I love this notebook and use it daily now. Thanks Chris. See http://jackcheng.com/stuff-i-love-muji-chronotebook

- **Take a poll**. I've asked people how often they like to see posts on Zen Habits, things they want me to write about, whether I should do a Zen Habits post about the presidential election, and other similar poll questions, and have gotten some great feedback

- **Tell people interesting things**. If you have something going on in your life that's really interesting, by all means, share it. That's what Twitter is about. It often gets some great conversations going. If you don't have anything interesting to say, don't be afraid to be silent. No one really cares if you don't say anything, but it's annoying to read people share things that aren't interesting.

- **Jump into conversations sometimes**. I don't think you should get involved in every conversation, but sometimes it can be fun to jump in and say your two cents. Then jump back out when you're done.
- **Find some great reading**. When I feel like a distraction and want to read something useful or interesting, I'll scan through my Twitter stream and find a few cool links to read. People share some really great stuff from the web on Twitter. However, as a warning, it can be overwhelming if you try to read everything. Again, it's a river — go into the water when you feel like it, but get back out too — don't try to consume the entire river.

- **Learn to be concise**. What I really love about Twitter is its 140 character limit for tweets. Some people cheat by doing multiple tweets about the same thing, but that defeats the purpose of the limit. Instead, learn to say just the essential in one post (or two if you really need to). It forces you to choose, to edit, to simplify. I love that. I wish email had a limit

- **Use it as a log**. I forget where I read this idea, but one fitness blogger suggested using Twitter to help lose weight: post *everything* you eat on Twitter. It's a great idea (I think it was Craig Ballantyne) because it hold you accountable, and you don't want to post something that you shouldn't have eaten. But Twitter could be used as a workout log, a travelogue, anything really.

- **Find someone to hire**. Just now I posted on Twitter to find someone to redo the software for Guampedia.com in Drupal or Joomla. Got some great responses already! Whoever you need to find, Twitter should be able to help

- **Reduce your inboxes**. If you use Twitter regularly, you can probably reduce your need for RSS (my favorite blogs are on Twitter anyways), email (you can DM people), IM, news sites, and so on. It's nice to consolidate, as long as you use it intelligently.

- **Create a Twitter personal assistant**. Check out this guide for a pretty cool use of Twitter and associated services. http://grinding.be/2008/02/25/more-notes-on-presence-how-to-stay-in-contact-when-youre-everywhere/

Just for fun: check out Twittervision 3D for an incredible global representation of tweets at they happen around the globe in real time.

Cyber Minimalist: How to Work (Almost) Completely Online

A couple of days ago, I did a little post that mentioned how I don't use my hard drive to store my files, and that all my files are online. Well, that drew so much interest that I've decided to provide more detailed information on the topic.

In the past year, I've decided to simplify my computing life and my work needs by trying to work, as much as possible, with online apps and online storage.

I was tired of emailing myself files between home and work computers, or uploading files to web storage and syncing them between computers, or loading them onto flash drives. I'd forget where a file was, I'd spend a lot of time transferring files and organizing things, my two computers were never completely in sync, and it was just too complicated for a minimalist like myself.

Enter online apps, and my newfound simplicity.

Now, my computing life is much simpler than ever before. I use online apps as much as possible — admittedly, my needs are much simpler than most people's needs, but that's intentionally so, as I've learned that most of the stuff I did was not essential. I've slowly reduced my needs, so that online apps can take care of the majority of what I do.

When Online Computing Would Work For You

I must stress that this online solution I've been using is not for everyone. It may not meet your needs. If not, move on — I'm not saying everybody should follow what I'm doing.

But there might be some who would benefit from online solution. Here are some reasons you'd store your files online and use online apps:

- **You use multiple computers**. If you carry a laptop everywhere, then you don't have the problem of transferring or syncing files. But if you have more than one computer, you might consider my solution.

- **Your needs are simple**. If you use desktop software that cannot be replaced by online apps, my solution is probably not for you. You might still consider online storage. If you're a writer, however, or you deal mostly with word processing apps, spreadsheets, and other common apps, you might be able to get away with what I do.

- **You do a lot of online work**. If you're a blogger, like I am, or some other type of web worker, and you meet the criteria above, online solutions would be perfect for you.

My Online Solution – How I Work

Let me stress, again, that this is my solution. Your needs will be different. You will want to alter your solution to fit your needs. But I offer the following as an example of how you could work online with a minimalist approach to computing:

1. **Word processing and spreadsheets**. It wasn't long ago when I did a little analysis of my work and realized that the majority of it was done with word processors such as MS Word and AbiWord, and spreadsheets such as Excel or Calc. I decided to try using Google Docs for these needs, and though it was a little off-putting at first, I've since learned to embrace the minimalism of Google Docs and Spreadsheets. They don't have half the features of their Microsoft counterparts, but you know what? I don't need those missing features. Formatting not as pretty? I've become all about the info, not the

formatting. Printing not as pretty? I rarely print now. And sharing docs with others is so much easier now.

2. **Blogging**. Of course, almost every blogger uses an online app for publishing his blog. I use Wordpress, and it's simple to use and powerful enough for my needs. I save a post, add a photo, and those things don't need to be saved on my hard drive.

3. **Photos**. I've embraced Google's Picasa, and uploaded all my photos onto my free Picasa account. Yes, I'm a Google freak, and others have problems trusting a company like Google, but I don't.

4. **Email**. This is one of my most heavily used apps. While in my last job we were required to use Outlook, I've since been freed to use Gmail, and I'll never go back. Boy is it so much nicer. And as I tend to clean out my Gmai every now and then, I doubt if I'll ever come close to the storage limit. The nice thing is that as soon as I email a file to someone, I can delete it from my hard drive, as it's now stored in Gmail.

5. **Archive and search**. This is one of the most beautiful reasons to use online apps: the simplicity of organization. While I used to have a structure of directories and subdirectories for the files on my hard drive (as nearly everyone does, I think), now I don't worry about folders or even tagging. I archive, and then search when I need a file. That's it. It works just as well in Gmail as Google Docs as Picasa as Wordpress. No need for filing. It took me awhile to get used to this method, but now I love it. Need to find a document I saved a few months ago? No need to root through folders to find it. Just search. It's beautiful.

6. **Desktop apps**. I do use desktop apps, for some work. For example, AbiWord or DarkRoom for minimal

word processing, Photoshop or Gimp for photo editing, AutoHotKey for keyboard shortcuts, some graphics programs, and some specialty apps for my day job. However, I usually use them for a single task, save the file, upload it or email it immediately, and then delete the file from my hard drive.

7. **No hard drive organization**. Again, as soon as I save a file my hard drive, I transfer it online (to Google Docs, Gmail, Picasa, Wordpress, etc.) and then delete it from the hard drive. This means that I no longer need to organize files on my hard drive. I still have my old files — I've been afraid to delete them, although I will probably do so within a couple of months. But no new files are kept on my hard drive.

8. **Firefox**. Of course, the desktop app I use the most is my browser. And for my money, that's Firefox. (Opera, Safari, Camino and other browser fans will disagree, and that's OK — this isn't a debate about the best browser.) Since I do almost all of my work online, Firefox is just about always open, and one thing I love is the shortcuts that give me fast computing all day long. I have keyword bookmarks for every app and site I use often, so opening up a site or app is as simple as typing a couple of letters and pressing enter. Same thing for my common searches on Wikipedia, Flickr, Amazon, IMDB, and much more — they all have very fast keywords, so searches are easy. And Firefox's extensions have helped me tremendously, including Greasemonkey, Google Toolbar, and more.

9. **Offline work**. There are times when I shut down Firefox and open a desktop app such as DarkRoom or AbiWord, just so I can work without the temptation of being connected. I find it peaceful to disconnect, and not have to worry about distractions. But when I'm

done with that task, such as writing an article, I'll save it into Google Docs and delete the original.

10. **Calendar and to-dos**. I use (surprise) GCal for my online calendar needs, and my to-dos have found a number of good online tools. (I've migrated between Backpack, Tracks, Vitalist, and others, depending on my mood. Right now, I'm using my Moleskine pocket notebook.) There are other online apps I use, most notable among them Google Reader.

Update: Frequently Asked Questions

There were a bunch of excellent questions in the comments that I thought I should address in the article itself, as many readers don't read all the comments, and I didn't want to have to deal with the same questions over and over.

1. **What about backups?** I don't actually do backups for the most part. All the companies I use to store my information online backup the information themselves. However, even if there were a problem, I wouldn't miss any of the information, really, except my blog. And I do backup my blog. However, if you wanted to backup your information, it wouldn't be hard to do it yourself — you could use your hard drive or web storage in a different location, and just save new or modified files every day or once a week.

2. **What about privacy?** This is a real issue for some people, and I won't deny it. However, I don't really think Google employees (or whatever company I'm using) have time to read through everyone's files, and even if they read mine, I don't have anything secret in my documents. If that's an issue for you, for whatever reason, online work would be more difficult. You could encrypt files — maybe only those that you really want to protect.

3. **Capture and calendaring when I'm not at my computer**. I use my Moleskine pocket notebook. I don't keep that many appointments — again, it's the minimalist in me. I might have one per day, and often less. I don't like to keep a full schedule, and I avoid meetings like the plague. I've developed a sort of judo technique to meetings. I do take meetings, but rarely. Anyway, you could use your cell phone or other mobile device to do calendaring on the go if you like.

4. **Being hostage to your Internet Provider**. This can also be a very real issue for some people. It hasn't seemed to be an issue for me. However, things are looking better on this front. With Google Gears, many web apps are soon going to have an off-line mode, so even if you get disconnected, you can continue to do your work. Zoho Office apps just got that capability, I believe.

5. **What's the objection to using the space on your hard drive?** None really, except for what I said near the beginning of the article: I use multiple computers, and I need to access the information from anywhere. Using online apps allows me to do that. Also, having my info online makes organization much easier (see discussion above about archive and search). There's no need for a central organizational structure anymore, whether you're using Google or Mac OSX.

6. **But what if not everything I do can be done online?** It's true that many apps are not offered online, and also that most online apps do not have all the features of desktop apps. First, this is why I simplified my needs — I've learned that I don't need all the features of desktop apps. Sure, MS Word has 27 million more features than Google Docs, and so does Excel, but I don't use them, and for me, they just add to bloat and slowness. For others who need them, the online solution wouldn't be ideal. Second, I do use desktop

apps for certain things, like photo editing, as I mentioned above. But then I upload the file online, delete the copy on my hard drive, and don't worry about it after that. Again, this might not work for everyone, but it works for me.

Final note: I should have had this in the original article, but here's the key issue: if working online would be more complicated for you, don't do it. For me, it has meant a simplification and minimalization of my computing life, and I really enjoy that minimalism. Others have more complicated needs, or have issues with privacy, backups, security or the quality of their connections. Those people shouldn't use an online solution, as I do, because it would be more complicated for them. And that's the final test — what is simpler and makes more sense for your situation?